"The Longest Time Stuck in an Elevator" and "The Shortest Street"
were first published in *Seeing the Blue Between: Advice and Inspiration to Young Poets*
by Paul Janeczko, Candlewick Press, 2000.

Records written about in this book are primarily from
The Guinness Book of World Records, various editions,
and may have changed since this book was written.

Book design by Sara Gillingham.
Typeset in Grit Primer.
The illustrations in this book were rendered in acrylic paints and colored pencils.
Manufactured in Hong Kong.

Library of Congress Cataloging-in-Publication Data
Lewis, J. Patrick.
The worlds greatest: poems / by J. Patrick Lewis; illustrated by Keith Graves.
p. cm.
ISBN 978-0-8118-5130-5
1. Children's poetry, American. I. Graves, Keith, ill. II. Title.
PS3562.E9465W47 2008
811'.54—dc22
2007014717

10 9 8 7 6 5 4 3 2 1

Chronicle Books LLC
680 Second Street, San Francisco, California 94107

www.chroniclekids.com

J. PATRICK LEWIS & KEITH GRAVES

present

THE WORLD'S GREATEST:

POEMS

chronicle books · san francisco

Contents

the Kookiest Hat

INVENTED BY RAYMOND D. KIEFER
SPRING CITY, PENNSYLVANIA, 1995

As I was walking down the street,
  I met a man who wore
A fried egg on his head. I said,
  "Dear me, what is it for?"

"A fried-egg hat repels the rain,"
  Was what the man replied,
"Because, my dear, I always wear
  It on the sunny side."

the Shortest Street

ELGIN STREET, BACUP, ENGLAND

Go take a walk
Down Elgin Street,
Where people talk
For seventeen feet.

"Good day!"

          "Hello!"

Is all they say—
Then turn, and go
The other way.

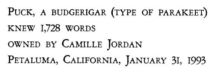

the Talkingest Bird

PUCK, A BUDGERIGAR (TYPE OF PARAKEET)
KNEW 1,728 WORDS
OWNED BY CAMILLE JORDAN
PETALUMA, CALIFORNIA, JANUARY 31, 1993

Unlike average chirping birds
(Nuthatch, cardinal and canary),
Puck preferred to utter words
Found in Webster's dictionary.

He talked all day till he was blue,
And even then he wasn't through.
He hardly stopped to sleep or play
Through February, March and May . . .

Though Puck began to mutter, sputter,
Whenever he ate pnnnut bttttr!

the Longest

 Traffic Jam

109.3 MILES LONG
LYONS TOWARD PARIS, FRANCE
FEBRUARY 16, 1980

Graphic
Traffic
Crawling
Stalling
Fender
Bender
Bumper
Thumper.
Temper,
Temper!
Beeping
(Bleeping!)
Creeping
Going
Slowing
Knowing
Weekend
Bleak end.

the Stone Skipping

WIMBERLEY, TEXAS
OCTOBER 20, 1991

The pebble made rough music,
Humming past a tiny
Island in the Blanco
River.
Touch tone, touch stone.
You could count the beats more or less

Evenly.
It was easy—
Guess
How many times
The pebble dimpled the water.

Record

ROSEBERG, OREGON
3 x 3¾ INCHES
1876

THE DAILY BANNER

Business section Funnies News
Crossword puzzle Book reviews
Here's who died   Latest sports
Want ads   Weekly farm reports
Weather (cloudy) Women's wear

The BANNER world's a 3-inch square!

The Longest Time a Message Was in a Bottle at Sea

RELEASED JUNE 12, 1914
ISLAND OF FOULA, SHETLAND ISLANDS, SCOTLAND
FOUND 5 MILES FROM THE RELEASE SITE
AUGUST 21, 1996

This is what you wrote
In that sea-swept note—
    June the 12th, 1914 ...
Inside a bottle submarine.

Sailor from the sea,
No biography
Bobbed up in the foam.
Hope you made it home.

the Tall-est Roll-er Coast-er

SUPERMAN THE ESCAPE
SIX FLAGS MAGIC MOUNTAIN
VALENCIA, CALIFORNIA
415-FOOT STEEL SUPPORT STRUCTURE

You're swerving north,
You're curving south,
Your stomach sits
Inside your mouth.

You hold your breath,
You lose your nerve,
You're scared to death
At every curve.

You're feeling very
Sick, but then
You tell your Dad,
"Let's go again!"

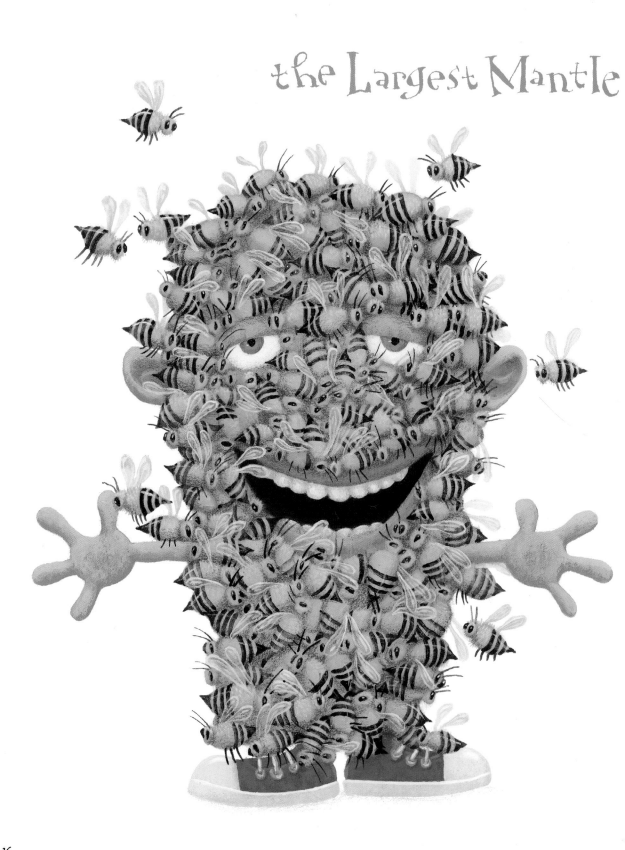

# of Bees

Jed Shaner, covered by a mantle of an estimated 343,000 bees
Staunton, Virginia
June 29, 1991

A busy buzzy body, he's
a hive for eighty pounds of bees.
His beard was bees,
his nose was bees,
his arms and legs and toes were bees.

His wife, they tell us, laughed so hard
she broke the hammock in the yard!
We don't know why it struck her funny,
but ever since, she's called him *Honey*!

the Shortest Snake

Thread snake
longest specimen 4 1/4 inches
Martinique, Barbados, and St. Lucia

"Who's the shortest snake in Snakedom?"
    said the Lizard to the Toad.
"Mrs. Thread Snake," Toady told him,
    "though she can't be stitched or sewed.

"She can squeeze inside a pencil
    if the lead's been taken out
for she isn't any bigger
    than the shadow of a doubt."

"Introduce me," said the Lizard,
    as he shimmied down the vine.
"If she's too small to eat lizards,
    she can be a friend of mine!"

the Dumbest Dinosaur

STEGOSAURUS ("PLATED LIZARD")
30 FEET LONG, 1.9 TONS
BRAIN WEIGHT 2½ OUNCES
LIVED 150 MILLION YEARS AGO

Clankety-clank, clankety-clank
Stegosaurus came roaming
Across the vast and blistered plains
Of what is now Wyoming.

Two tons of escalator plates!
The Stegosaur was gruesome—
You can count your blessings they
Do not still reproduce 'em.

The Steg was so ferocious, he
Could flatten any wall but
He had a Stego-simple brain
No bigger than a walnut!

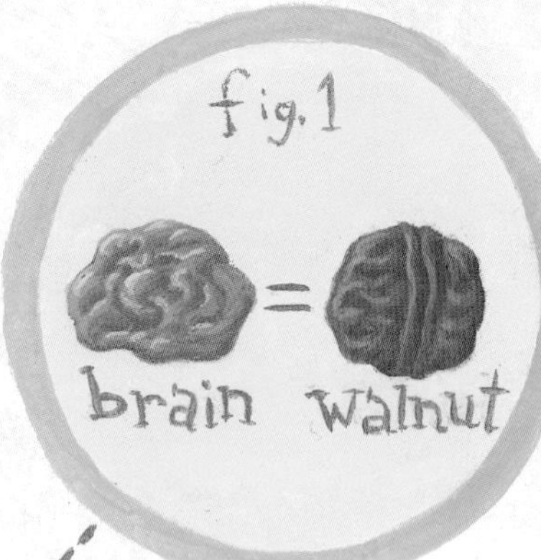

fig. 1

brain = walnut

18

the Tallest Christmas Tree

221 FEET
NORTHGATE SHOPPING CENTER
SEATTLE, WASHINGTON, DECEMBER 1950

★
A
tree
as tall
as that,
good sir,
would have
to be a Doug-
las fir. Now if all
children four feet
tall lay end to end
outside the mall, how
many would it take to
be as long as that great
Christmas tree? If you're
correct—land sake's alive!—
the
an-
swer's over
fifty-five!

the Most Kisses

ALFRED A. E. WOLFRAM
KISSED 10,504 PEOPLE IN EIGHT HOURS
MINNESOTA RENAISSANCE FESTIVAL
AUGUST 19, 1995

Wolfram, Alfred,
 super-duper
  pucker-upper,
   quicker smacker
    lipper-wiper
     merry-maker,
      kisser-swapper
       record breaker.

Wolfram, Alfred
 couldn't kiss
  just one Min-
   nesota miss,
    went and kissed
     10,000 more.
      (Somebody was
       keeping score.)

the Longest Time Stuck in an Elevator

MING KUANG CHEN,   BRONX, NEW YORK
TRAPPED IN AN ELEVATOR   FOR 81 HOURS, APRIL 1–5, 2005

It is quiet,   it is lonely
When you find   yourself the only
Population in   an elevator car.

It is spooky,   it is scary
When you are   the solitary
Population in   an elevator car.

It is drafty,   it is creepy
When you have   become one sleepy
Population in   an elevator car.

Three days later,   what a tingle
When at last   you're *not* the single
Population in   that elevator car!

the Most Plates Spinning

Dave Spathaky, London, England
108 plates, November 23, 1992

... plate **92**
knows what to do

(but **17**
begins to lean)

95
can stay alive

(but **41**
is almost done!)

99
is doing fine

(but look at poor
plate **24**!)

103
is worry-free

(but **36**
is in a fix)

plate **108** ...
a record!

WAIT!

(**44**
just hit the floor!)

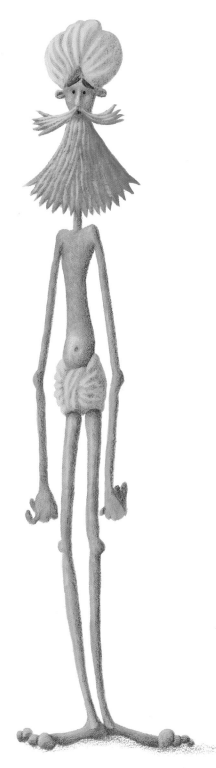

the Longest Time a Human Remained Standing

SWAMI MAUJGIRI MAHARAJ, 17 YEARS PERFORMING PENANCE
SHAHJAHANPUR, UTTAR PRADESH, INDIA, 1955–1973

A plank was where I leaned to sleep.
Years later, I remember it—
Day by day and bit by bit,
I had forgotten how to sit.

Time took its time—eternal sweep
Of sun and stars across the land.
I went without a helping hand
Until I let myself unstand.

the Tallest Scarecrow

"STRETCH II"
103 FEET 6 1/4 INCHES TALL
CONSTRUCTED BY THE SPEERS FAMILY
PARIS, ONTARIO, CANADA, SEPTEMBER 2, 1989

One hundred three and a half feet tall,
Stretch even made the barn look small.
He scared the crows and dwarfed the trees—
You couldn't even reach his knees.
He swatted clouds, directed jets,
And terrified the neighbors' pets.
The slightest breeze would up and blow
His sleeves across Ontario!

Somebody said, in Paris, France,

His giant shirt and long Stretch pants

Were flapping wildly—transatlantic!

The mayor's wife was simply frantic!

The Royal Canadian Mounted Police

Said, "Stretch must not disturb the peace!

By accident he might step on

Alberta
or
Saskatchewan!"

And so it went until the day
A six-year-old came out to say,
"Girls are made of skin and bones,
And boys are made of sticks and stones,
Cats and dogs are pelt and paw,
But Stretch is only made of straw."

the Biggest Potato

PLANTED BY PATRICK K. SLOANE, ISLE OF MAN
7 POUNDS 13 OUNCES, 1994

There once was a tater named Spud,
Who said to his tater tot, "Bud,
     Remember the size is
      What takes Tater Prizes,
So don't be a stick-in-the-mud!"

A Sonnet to the Greatest Distance Hang Gliding by a Woman

Kari Castle, 208.6 miles
Owens Valley, California, July 22, 1991

Man,
I
can
fly
my
blue
sky
to
see
more
sea-
shore
and
sand!

the Winningest Woman of the Iditarod Dog Sled Race

SUSAN BUTCHER (1956–2006), FOUR-TIME WINNER

I rode the whole Iditarod
From Anchorage to Nome!
The husky-sleigh, eleven-day
Iditarod to Nome.

Two moose can cause a traffic jam.
(There is no word in Moose for *"Scram!"*)
And over trails of ice and snow,
No musher knows which way to go.
The weather? Forty-two below
Could freeze the whiskers in a beard!
The huskies up front disappeared.
And though it sounds a little weird—
Okay, you're right, extremely odd—
I did, I *did* Iditarod—
A bitter cold Iditarod—
My sled slid the Iditarod
From Anchorage to Nome.

the Biggest Pumpkin

Grown By Larry Checkon, North Cambria, Pennsylvania
1,469 pounds, October 1, 2005

The pumpkin must have been
    Invented by a child
Who thought the world could use
    A vegetable that smiled.

the Crookedest Building

As it was built
(not yet complete)
this structure tilt-
ed seventeen feet.
And now each cit-
izen of Pisa's
p r a y i n g i t
survives the breezes.

the Most Live Scorpions Eaten by a Human

RENÉ ALVARENGA
35,000 (OR 20 TO 30 PER DAY)
INTIPUKA, EL SALVADOR

In Intipuka town there lives a gentleman, René,
Who's most particular about the beef on his buffet.
He eats a dozen scorpions for breakfast, then for lunch
Another dozen. Says René, "They're better by the bunch.

"A creature so disgusting is a delicacy grand!"
(A delicacy other Intipukans cannot stand.)
"A spider? Much too stringy. Bad tarantula can sicken.
And yet a hairy scorpion can taste a lot like chicken.

"I lick its tiny drumsticks off, then bite its lobster claw,
And save its tail for my dessert—I eat the fellow raw.
A scorpion still kicking makes a lively dinner!" Still,
It has a way of making other Intipukans ill.

the Most Cobras Kissed Consecutively

GORDON CATES OF ALACHUA, FLORIDA
KISSED II MONOCLE COBRAS AND A 15-FOOT KING COBRA
LOS ANGELES, CALIFORNIA, SEPTEMBER 25, 1999

When a cobra gives you the stare,

                  beware!

When a cobra wants to attack,

                  stand back.

When a cobra gives you a chill,

                  be still.

When you give a cobra a kiss . . .

                  Don't miss!

the Highest Air on a Skateboard

DANNY WAY, NEAR AGUANGA, CALIFORNIA
JUNE 19, 2003, 23 1/2 FEET BACKSIDE AIR (ON A QUARTERPIPE)

I seized the sudden sky
        like the cool Concorde
On witchy wonder wheels
        of my boomerang board
Past pop-eyed people pointing
        at the disappearing dart
Of a shin-skinned skimmer
        off the champions' chart!